THE VICIOUS ROSE

By Seth Sorrell

The Vicious Rose by Seth Sorrell

Published By Seth Sorrell

Website: https://sethemountain.wordpress.com

Copyright © 2024 by Seth Sorrell

All rights reserved.

ISBN Number(Paperback): 9798878460354

No part of this publication may be reproduced, distributed, or transmitted in any form or by any means, including photocopying, recording, or other electronic or mechanical methods, without the publisher's prior written permission, except as permitted by U.S. copyright law. For permission requests, contact Seth Sorrell at seththemountain@gmail.com.

The story, all names, characters, and incidents portrayed in this production are fictitious. No identification with actual persons (living or deceased), places, buildings, and products is intended or should be inferred.

Book Cover and Editing by Seth Sorrell

First Edition 2024

Table of Contents

Foreword *1*
The Vicious Rose *2*
The Vicious Muse *3*
High Expectations *4*
The Dues of the Accomplished *5*
Freyja and Tyr *6*
Enter Stage, Exit Stage *7*
Don't Envy a Whole Heart *8*
Bicycle *9*
Beloved *10*
Beloved Brother *11*
To My Lost Brothers *12*
Amelia *13*
A Coward's Heart *14*
Asher in Ashes *15*
Guardian Mother *16*
Troubled Father *17*
The Elders *18*
Defeated Family *19*
Disturbed Streetlight *20*
Heartbreaker's Confession *21*

Here I Die Again	22
Open House	23
Indecision	24
Plagued	25
Reduce Me to Ash	26
Selling Myself	27
To the Lonely Man	28
Unveil	29
No Happy Ending	30
Walked Out	31
The Duality of the Mountain	32
V for Victory	33
Farewell, You Vicious Rose	34
Words I've Left Behind	35
Acknowledgments	36
About The Mountain	37
Connect With The Mountain	38

Foreword

     Life, by its nature, is duality. Human propensity is to seek/accept that which we call good, to shun that which we deem bad. We appreciate the rose's beauty but dread the thorn's prick. It is incongruous to our sensibilities that the most beautiful thing may also be the most savage. In, The Vicious Rose, poet Seth Sorrell explores many of life's juxtapositions.

     The natural world in contrast to our emotional existence. We chase the elusive as the wind; yet, when we capture it, the elusive often offers us only emptiness. Sorrell explores concepts of angst, brokenness, fear, loss, heartbreak. In his poetry, Sorrell speaks of pain, but in speaking of pain, offers us hope and restoration. He challenges us to question our motivations for our behaviors. Chides us to be all in, particularly when it comes to love. Using the metaphor of the rose, the poet offers us the bright crimson beauty of the flower while reminding us of the brown edges of reality. Enjoy these poems as an adventure into the deeper consciousness of your being.

     John Hinton, President
     Poetry Society of Indiana.

Dedicated to Tami and Norman

The Vicious Rose

Roses are nature's affectionate feelings,
painted across the Earth's gardens.
Roses are commonly seen,
but few times, felt.
The Rose does wonders,
for those who breathe its scent,
but for those inexperienced with the scent,
what is left is lament.
The love of the Rose
is vicious.

The Vicious Muse

The Vicious Rose is a poet's muse.
Heartache is the ultimate tool to inspire,
but unless tempered, it will devour.

High Expectations

The day's coming soon.
I've anticipated it,
as a fisherman,
anticipates his next catch.
Yet,
when the day came,
It wasn't a fish story.

On this day,
I expected my hopes,
to shine brighter,
than the noon sun.
Instead,
they were shrouded,
by the cloudy midnight moon.

Beware of high hopes.
If they come true,
as you wish,
you join the luxurious minority.
When they stay fantasy,
as you fear,
you remain,
in the impoverished majority.

The Dues of the Accomplished

All these accolades, but emptiness remains.
All this praise, but the vicious rose is unabated.
You can reign supreme, but solemn it will seem.

Freyja and Tyr

Freyja's spirit lives in my mind.
I remember when I aided the brokenhearted
with my stanzas and proverbs.
I remember when I lifted
those whose souls were broken down
to the mountaintop.
I think my love is pure,
or may it just be vicious?

Tyr's spirit lords over my heart.
Those who loved me, those who were indifferent,
remember the times I said I'd heal them,
only for me to mortally infect them.
They remember when I abandoned them,
just when the winds began their furious cry.
I think my viciousness is truly me,
but is it me completely?

Freyja and Tyr
battle for complete domination of my essence.
My mind wants to hand out roses,
but my heart wants to strike sword blows.
The one who wins will only be revealed,
when before Odin I kneel.

Enter Stage, Exit Stage

Enter stage left,
I arrived.
You looked at me,
welcomingly.
We would sweep the awards,
with our believable performance.
My dear,
you had our audience fooled,
if only I had realized,
I, too, was just a spectator.

I tried to invest in you,
but by inflating my hopes,
I would only make,
A bigger explosion.

Exit stage right,
I leave.
Our production
has ended its run.
Even though I'm replaced,
if the script isn't revised,
the explosions,
will make a crater in your stage.

Don't Envy a Whole Heart

The ones with a whole heart retain childhood bliss.
Their struggle is an ice sheet, not an iceberg.
The ones with a whole heart lack motivation for growth.
The ones whose heart is made into jigsaw pieces,
must grow to form a new puzzle.

The ones with a shattered heart can aid the beaten down,
while the ones with a whole heart are perplexed by a frown.

Bicycle

Two wheels, chained together.
One to lead, the other to guide.
Both so entwined neither could break.

It arrived with a promise.
Liberation. Exaltation.
A new path.

Distance offered loose bolts,
broken handles,
no semblance of control.

Hopes were dashed as it
fell to pieces. So now,
I will walk.

Beloved

Beloved, I see you in every failed endeavor.
One year slips away
like your hand after an embrace.

Beloved, I remain solid, a statue,
solemn against your shapeless frivolity.
And still I yearn for your glance,
no matter how hexed with dread, how my bliss is fleeing.

Beloved, I see our jagged reflection
pieces that cannot align,
and they have left me scarred.
Yet still, I picture us whole.

Beloved, I beg the Almighty for peace,
but my anger holds its own leash.
I want to dethrone you, to cut the ties,
end your reign over my mind.
But how can one man throw a coup?

Beloved Brother

My beloved brother has bent my trust.
He couldn't tolerate the burning sun of my future,
So, my brother made my perception an icy moon.
The blinding destroyed bridges with the truthful,
and only multiplied my despair.

That beloved brother is a bastard.
He was a brother by our bond,
but now he is a spirit of the past.

To My Lost Brothers

A man needs brotherhood
to show him true masculinity
defined by strength in mind and body
and compassion to those
facing hellish fury.

A brother won't leave you to face
that fury isolated and in fear.
A brother would try to bring peace
when his fellow brothers are at odds.

I'm a man lacking brotherhood
cynical to its true masculinity
defined by abrasion in mind, tyranny in body,
and callousness to those fighting hell's forces.

All my brothers leave me isolated and fearful.
My brothers pick sides,
the side most convenient to them.

The embrace of a woman may momentarily
warm a man's soul,
but the hold of a brother heals his soul.

Amelia

During an uneventful morning,
I sat in a London Cafe alone.
The sky radiated azure.
The coffee, the fuel to my pulse,
and the power to my stampeding thoughts.
In a moment,
my day would change.

She floated in, a spirit, a breathtaking change
in a single moment.
Amelia.
She was enchanting.
Her eyes could cast a spell, her face possessed me.

She took my hand,
and in just a moment
the day belonged to her.

We toured museums,
guided by her hand.
We had shared a pint, shared a meal,
shared our interests.
In just one moment,
we shared our lives.

To Amelia,
no more than a memory now,
it might have been love.
Or maybe, it was just one moment.

A Coward's Heart

Taken to my limits with the task at hand,
I surrendered to indifference.
In this concession,
I failed those who gazed upon my marble bust.

How can I create prophesies
of becoming someone great,
when I lack the will to endure?

How can I love myself,
when I make decisions,
which bring my visions to ruin?

The truth is this,
I cannot fulfill great prophesies,
when I have a coward's heart.
I cannot love myself,
when I have a coward's heart.

Asher in Ashes

King Asher overlooks the balcony.
Behold, in the bath, an enchantress.
The King's desire doesn't decide his action.
Instead, it's his lunar behavior.
The King's anxiety burns brightly.

Love left King Asher's bliss beaten blue
and his relationships rusted.
The King was told to make himself greater.
So, he acquired enough books to run a printing press.
He transformed his gluttonous diet into a fast.
King Asher burned like Greek fire.

This transformation was done in vain.
Asher couldn't find love,
not because his worth was invisible to the world,
but because it wasn't apparent to his lunar mind.

Asher breaks every mirror,
reflecting his vulnerable armor
and cynical amour.
He could have been transfigured,
but his darkness merely transformed.
Asher lies like one in the womb.
He lies in royal ashes.

Guardian Mother

I knew I didn't have her long enough,
When I could no longer remember her voice.
The voice that soothed my beaten spirit
has evaporated like fog.

When the bottle consumed my father,
my mother shielded me from his trouble.
Inevitably, my guard fell,
plunging me deep into a hellish spell.

My mother looks down upon me,
assured that her son has healed.
Knowing the vicious rose will stare at me,
but will never have a hold.

Troubled Father

The fermented odor haunts my childhood,
like the former touchdown glories
of a man trapped in adolescence.

When that foolish backwoodsman
collided with my father, wounds weren't just traded,
it was also the bottle sickness.

The vicious rose touched my father.
Not through a silver-tongued enchantress,
but through the bottle's melancholic lust.

My father's blissful spirit
has long since fled his drunken body.
Maybe when I see him again,
we can trade an embrace, not a wound.

The Elders

I'm told to honor my elders,
but when they invalidate my humanity,
I'm expected not to indulge in volcanity.

Defeated Family

In a family of defeated, slaying each other down.
Among the slain was a battered boy.

When his father was drinking oceans
and causing crushing whirlpools,
the defeated family stood aside.
When the boy asked for intervention,
they called him ungrateful for Father's provision.

When the boy found a calm stream,
The family acted happy,
but hid daggers of envy.

The boy has become a man with accolades.
The defeated family still slay themselves.
When they tried to take him back,
the man left the defeated repelled.

Disturbed Streetlight

In the distant, disturbed streetlight,
I see a boy battered by time.
A man, I presume his father,
stands like a redwood over him.
Verbal daggers burst the boy's spirit.
The boy has slash scars on his arm,
from vicious duels.

How could a boy,
with a supernova's flame in his being
be allowed such torment?

I step inside the streetlight,
to be blinded by mirror bulbs.
The boy battered by time
resides in my mind.
The verbal daggers, my affirmations.
The slash scars from duels with myself.
Who is the abusive father?
The one before my eyes.

Heartbreaker's Confession

I apologize to you, old friend.
When you wanted me free from depression throes,
I handed you a vicious rose.

Here I Die Again

Here I die again,
another lover's fog faded by my reality's rays.
Every lost love is the hangman's noose,
choking my faith in the rose,
and planting seeds of cynicism in Earth's gardens.

As I am suspended, limp
The Game Masters rejoice in glee,
for every lost love adds a new level
in their manipulative game.
I'm the ultimate entertainment
for a crowd of vicious wolves.

Here I die again,
and again, death brings no rest.
I'm killed and resurrected for eternity.
Heartache's knife plunges forcefully.

Open House

June's sun rays can mask deceptive smirks.
Riding the church's elevator,
I beam with the anticipation of your embrace.

Her family is proud of her accomplishments.
I mingle amongst them, prideful.
Indeed, I'm her best choice.
I can counteract her savage nature,
with pleasing madness.

It ends with a single picture of
that woman's head, nuzzling my shoulder.
What an adorable pair of youthful dreamers.
Now, her accomplished dream is visible on my screen.
My accomplished dream is yet to be seen.

Indecision

Half a year passes,
and still,
your essence infects,
the wound,
in my insular cortex.

I'm tempted to reach you,
but given,
whom I knew you to be,
you'll return my reach
to the sender.
Indeed, you haven't changed?

Do I embrace you,
or do I exclude you?
I long for your warmth,
but I forsake your burning savagery,
that you passed unto me.

If I could return,
to our time,
I wouldn't have sat on the fence.
I'd have made my claim,
and you'd claim me.

Plagued

In a short time, I could feel,
Thor's drumbeat
in your chest when we spoke.
Even though
we're so close,
The vicious specter still plagues me.

That hag of a specter.
The one that discarded me like a wilted rose.
She makes every new woman,
a cautious prospect.
Tell me,
are my cautions about you valid?

Don't use my affection
just to become vicious.
Don't lead me to love
to make my bitterness a chasm.
Be my lover or be my enemy.
Just choose one,
and let it be known to me.

Reduce Me to Ash

I lie in bed again,
saying how I'll be a stronger man.
I'll be more secure,
I'll be stable for her,
and the chemistry will remain electric.
She won't become an apparition.

I love that woman,
even if the feeling is numb.
With excess affection,
I try to make my neurons burn.
In reality,
the chemistry dissipates in smoke.

I tell you the truth,
The love I hold
extinguishes human patience.
No guru's advice will heal it.
No isolation can freeze it.
My love burns the world
and reduces me to ash.

Selling Myself

With my pressed suit,
and predictable pitch,
I go to your door
to sell me to you.

I'm a gentleman
with a brutish side.
I'm a working man
with a burnout's past.
I'm an extrovert
with an introvert's anxiety.

If you hesitate to buy me
due to my downgrades,
I'll cover them up
with overt affection.
I'll be so generous
that generosity itself
will be as tired to you
as an aged mule's eyes.

With a secured lock,
and silence,
I go to the next door.
I never learn
why all locks before
were secured
when I sell myself.

To the Lonely Man

My brother,
love does not exist for the likes of you and I.
Our passion
freezes the curiosity
others have in us.

My brother,
love does not exist for the likes of you and I.
Our aspirations
direct our decisions,
and any attempt towards renewal
is met with routine.

Unveil

I picture us
in a perfect embrace.
I imagine us
in a perfect connection.

My expectation is a portrait,
the reality a photograph.
The truth is cruel,
in unveiling the curtain.

The unveiling wounded me,
but living this way still,
would end me.

No Happy Ending

Guys like me don't get a happy ending.
When you're born to tragedy,
by tragedy, you will die.
When your life
has a desperate gambler's luck,
you don't get the luxury of a royal send-off.
Either you're shot and dumped in a hole,
or topping yourself off is a completed goal.

Walked Out

I've walked out so much,
my feet burn
like the eyes of those I left behind.
They all miss me, they all curse my name,
but my selfishness isn't to blame,
sometimes to choose your peace
means to choose chaos for others,
but in choosing my peace,
I concede my love for the left behind.

Am I going to walk out on you?
Am I going to learn to stick it out?
If I walk out on you,
you'd find peace,
but you'd concede what you hold dear.
If I stick it out,
night would reign on us for a time,
but in time,
the sun would shine once more,
for you and I.

The Duality of the Mountain

I'm desperate,
I'm a hustler.
I'm kind,
I'm a bastard.

All these terms and more,
define your vision of me.
What if all these terms
peacefully coexist?
What if I'm not the knight,
but not the vandal?

I'm a high-value man,
but not enough to be your lover.
I'm your brother,
but a joke said to your inner circle.

I'm the cause of your disgusted look,
but the curiosity in your mind.
You disrespect me,
but you aspire to match my energy.

The duality is what makes me a mountain,
not a hill.
The duality may make me insane,
but it will drive me to the extraordinary,
while you stroll to the ordinary.

V for Victory

The cursed shadow of the Vicious Rose
has been victorious for an age,
but my victorious era commences now.

I've seen death brought by the Vicious Rose.
It left me suspended limp, hanging in my chosen agony,
just to be resurrected for execution again.
I seemed to have neglected this fact,
I alone choose to pull the hangman's lever.

The cursed shadow of the Vicious Rose
has been victorious for an age,
but my victorious era commences now.

I can have the pain of that rose without being tortured.
I can choose the love of the attentive
and abandon seeking the love of the absent.
I can make the Earth's gardens beautiful again.

The cursed shadow of the Vicious Rose
has been victorious for an age,
but my victorious era commences now.

So, I flip the inverted peace sign to the Vicious Rose.
I make that sign for victory,
and to insult the reverence I've bestowed it.

The cursed shadow of the Vicious Rose
has been victorious for an age,
but my victorious era commences now.

Farewell, You Vicious Rose

Farewell, You Vicious Rose.
It's been two years
since the lovely morning we had.
We were both vicious,
but kind to the other.
Then our vicious thorns, pricked each other,
bled each other.

I'd be a liar if I said I didn't miss
how you made a black-hearted boy
a smirking mess.

Now I've got a lovely garden
where you once bloomed.
I'm the man I told you I'd become,
I hope you're a wholesome rose
in your own lovely garden.

Now the endlessly played tape frays,
and now I boldly run into a new fray.

Words I've Left Behind

Don't dwell on my death.
When I'm told well done,
don't replay my final breath.

Don't see me as selfish,
don't see me as an idol,
when all I was,
was a wounded thief,
who stole your heart,
and needed to be released.

Acknowledgments

I first want to thank the Lord Jesus Christ. He has provided me hope with every heartache. In times of loss and rejection, he has given me a reason to wake up in the morning. If it were not for his teachings and the hope he has given me, I may not have been able to make this book. I want to thank the Kokomo Tribune for featuring my first book, *From the Mountain,* in an article. They have done a wonderful job in helping Kokomo's writers get exposure. I look forward to working with them more in the future. I want to thank John Hinton and the rest of the Poetry Society of Indiana for giving Hoosier poets like-minded fellowship. I appreciate how they have emceed open mic nights in Kokomo, giving my hometown's poets a place to perform publicly.

I thank my grandparents, Joe and Hazel, for being present in every heartbreak and loss I've faced. We have had several hills and valleys in our relationships with each other, but they have stayed loyal to me. I want to thank my friends who are fellow creatives. Having such lovely friends who are ambitious with their art drives me as I drive them. My creative friends and I will find our place in the sun. Lastly, thank you, the reader, for purchasing and reading this book. I am grateful for your support. I hope that this book has been able to connect with the pains you've faced. The Vicious Rose can prick our hearts, but our hearts must heal.

Never let The Vicious Rose take you on a cold, bleak night.

About The Mountain

Seth "The Mountain" Sorrell is a writer based in Indiana.
He released his debut poetry book,
From the Mountain, in 2023.
Sorrell is a 2022 Indiana Poetry Ourselves State Finalist.

Connect With The Mountain

LinkTree: https://linktr.ee/seththemountain

Made in the USA
Middletown, DE
16 November 2024

64295597R00027